HOW TO DRAW
CARTOONS

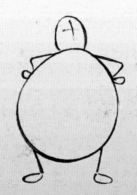

First published by Bardfield Press in 2006
Copyright © 2006 Miles Kelly Publishing Ltd

Bardfield Press is an imprint of
Miles Kelly Publishing Ltd,
Bardfield Centre, Great Bardfield, Essex, CM7 4SL

2 4 6 8 10 9 7 5 3 1

British Library Cataloguing-in-Publication Data
A catalogue record for this book is available from the British Library

ISBN 1-84236-557-6

Printed in China

Publishing Director: Anne Marshall
Editorial Director: Belinda Gallagher
Art Director: Jo Brewer
Editor: Rosalind McGuire
Designer: Tom Slemmings
Picture Research Manager: Liberty Newton
Picture Researcher: Laura Faulder
Production: Elizabeth Brunwin
Reprographics: Anthony Cambray
Mike Coupe, Stephan Davis, Ian Paulyn

www.mileskelly.net
info@mileskelly.net

HOW TO DRAW
CARTOONS

Author
Lisa Regan

Artist and consultant
Mike Foster at the Maltings Partnership

BARDFIELD
PRESS

Contents

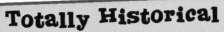

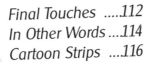

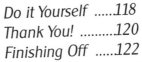

How to use...

Have a go!
Places to test out your ideas, and find examples and tips.

HAVE A GO!

Can you tell what it is about these animals that makes them look as though they are moving? Try drawing your own examples using these techniques.

On the Move

You could practise drawing animals standing around until the cows come home, but for real cartoons you'll need to set them in motion. Like people, you can move their arms, legs and heads and add action lines.

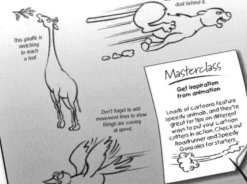

This cheetah is moving so fast it's leaving clouds of dust behind it.

This giraffe is stretching to reach a leaf.

Don't forget to add movement lines to show things are moving at speed.

Masterclass

Get inspiration from animation

Loads of cartoons feature speedy animals, and they're great for tips on different ways to put your cartoon critters in action. Check out Roadrunner and Speedy Gonzales for starters.

Animal Antics 79

78

A sketching section at the back lets you practise your new-found skills. The sketch book starts on page 124.

Masterclass
Projects and ideas to try out on your own.

Your book contains a library of cartoons to give you extra inspiration. The library is divided into sections by subject. Turn to page 44 for the first library.

Introduction

So, you want to learn to draw cartoons?
Are you really sure you've got what it takes?

Do you have eyes to copy what you see
around you? Are you able to hold a pencil?
Then you've got what it takes!

It also helps if you like watching people and
animals to see how they behave, to have a
sense of humour (or at least, a lighthearted
way of looking at life) and a little bit of
artistic flair. Don't worry too much about
those last three, though – this book intends
to teach you the last one, and you can
acquire the first two through
practice and observation.

So what are you waiting for?
Let's draw!

What is a Cartoon?

When you hear people talking about cartoons, you instantly get an image in your head of a certain kind of drawing. You know it's not going to be a portrait like the *Mona Lisa*, or a landscape with a realistic painting of what the artist saw.

Usually, cartoons involve people or animals, and they're often intended to be funny. They simplify what the artist wants to show you. Way back when people were drawing on their cave walls, they were starting a tradition of cartoons. Their pictures were simplistic, telling stories without getting bogged down in detail.

↑
Ancient cave art implies the shape and movement of an animal using only a few lines.

Cartoons often take one feature of their subject and exaggerate it to make you laugh, or to make a strong point. Political cartoons appeared in newspapers as long ago as the 1700s, and are still used today to draw attention to the amusing things that politicians and famous people get up to.

Screen Legends

The most famous types of cartoons are comic strips and animated cartoon stories. The first animated character was called Felix the Cat, introduced in silent movies in 1919.

Early cartoons were in black and white, with no talking. In 1928, a young man called Walt Disney introduced the world to a cartoon character called Mickey Mouse. The cartoons were a huge success, delighting audiences around the world.

Two of the world's most famous animal characters are Tom and Jerry. They've been around since the 1940s, and helped to launch the TV careers of their animators, William Hanna and Joseph Barbera. The Hanna–Barbera team took the duo to TV in the 1970s, and have created many other favourites, like the *Flintstones*, *The Powerpuff Girls* and *Scooby Doo*.

The antics of the mischievious mouse Jerry and the hapless cat Tom have been delighting audiences for over 60 years.

Shaggy and his dog Scooby Doo have been making viewers laugh at their hopeless ghost-hunting since 1969.

Early cartoons were all drawn by hand, with talented artists redrawing the characters over and over again. It takes roughly 24 different pictures (called frames) to make one second of cartoon animation.

Read all About It

From the 1930s onwards, cartoon strips became widespread, and early cartoon characters started to take on new forms.

Superheroes were great subjects for cartoons, because the only limit to the storylines was the writer's and artist's imagination. DC Comics produced many stories featuring superheroes, such as Superman and Batman.

Publications such as *The Beano* and *Dandy* are very obviously drawn in a different style to the DC comics, and instead of thrilling their readers with adventures, they aim to make them laugh with ridiculous characters and humorous storylines.

↑

Superman was the first comic book superhero to be created by Jerry Siegel and Joe Shuster, who went on to produce Batman and Wonderwoman.

Many cartoonists refer to 'cels' (short for 'celluloid' – a clear plastic that used to be used in animation). These are sheets with the main moving characters drawn on them. They are placed over the top of the backgrounds so the background only has to be drawn once.

New and Improved

Today many cartoons are taking advantage of brilliant new technology. Computers allow cartoonists to draw a single character and easily reproduce it hundreds of times, or to draw the outlines by hand and then colour them using computer graphics. Many cartoons look hand-drawn, but are created on computers.

Computers also allow artists to create characters in 3-D. Movies such as *Toy Story*, *Shrek* and *Finding Nemo* were all produced on computers, and look very different to cartoons that have been drawn by hand.

Some cartoons, such as *The Simpsons*, are still created by hand. The actual drawings and animation in *The Simpsons* are quite simplistic, but each episode still takes a huge team of people and a long time to make.

It can take six to nine months to write, record and draw up a single episode of **The Simpsons.**

Even with all the advantages of computer technology, the animation work for the movie **Shrek 2** *still took almost five years to complete.*

It's not just animated cartoons that are drawn on computers. Many illustrators now use computers to create 3-D pictures to illustrate books or packaging.

Back to Basics

Now you know a bit about the history of cartoons, it's time to fill you in on some of the basic skills and techniques that will get you drawing.

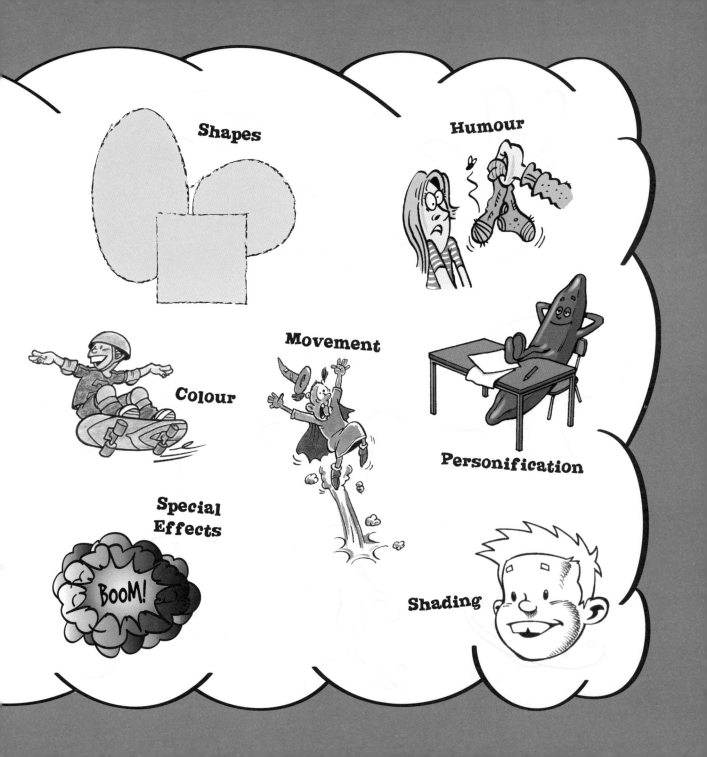

Shapes

Humour

Movement

Colour

Personification

Special
Effects

BooM!

Shading

Equipment

If you decide you want to try your hand at drawing cartoons, don't race out and spend lots of money on posh equipment. Most of what you need will be in your pencil case already. Find out first if you're going to enjoy cartooning, and if you have a talent for it!

Paper

Practise doodling characters on scrap paper. Copy your favourites into a notebook with unlined paper. Make the most of the practice pages in this handbook, too.

Coloured Pencils

Your cartoons will look much better coloured in. Use coloured pencils instead of felt-tips for a softer colour that doesn't look patchy and rough.

Pencil

The harder your pencil, the harder it is to rub out. Start with an ordinary HB or something a little softer, like a B or 2B.

Masterclass

Warming up

Draw a page full of circles and ovals to loosen your wrist and get used to the feeling of pencil on paper.

Pens

Many cartoonists draw in pencil but then use black ink to go over the outline. Black felt-tip is fine for this – experiment with fat ones and thin ones for different effects. You'll also need a good quality ink pen to write neatly in your speech bubbles.

Sharpener

Sharpen your pencils to a point (most school sharpeners are fine) then scribble on scrap paper to make the end rounded instead of scratchy.

Ruler

Your pictures won't need hard, straight lines, but you may need to divide your page into boxes for cartoon strips.

Tracing Paper

This is sometimes handy if you're drawing the same scene or character over and over again.

Now all I need is inspiration...

Eraser

If you practise before you do your final drawings, you shouldn't need to rub things out much. When you do, use a soft, clean, white eraser.

Style Guide

Although 'cartoon' makes you think of a certain style of picture that is very different from a portrait or a traditional landscape painting, there are many different ways of drawing a cartoon. Take a look at these pages and see for yourself. Some of the styles are drawn in different ways. Sometimes, they're just coloured in different ways.
Once you start to draw your own cartoons, you'll be able to see what style you're best at.

Digital

This cartoon bear was created on a computer. The light makes him look almost 3-D.

Flat Colour

Many cartoons use black outlines with flat colours inside. This lion was hand drawn as an outline and then scanned onto a computer to add colour.

Hand-drawn

Here, the colour was added by hand. The artist's style is to leave some areas uncoloured to add to the cartoony feel.

Watercolour

This elephant has been drawn as a black ink outline, and then coloured using watercolour paints.

Comic

Superhero cartoons have a very different style. The people are exaggerated to make them larger than life, rather than funny. Some cartoonists specialize in this kind of drawing.

Sketch

This is the simplest form of cartoon. If you can sketch like this and make people laugh, you have a special talent!

Manga

Manga-style cartoons originated in Japan. They tend to emphasize line, and the characters often have large eyes.

Humour

This book will try to teach you the basic techniques needed to draw funny cartoons. If you want to draw in a different style, like superheroes, you need to study those sort of comic books for your inspiration. Drawing funny cartoons isn't easy – for starters, how do you make people laugh at them?

Some cartoons exaggerate real life to make people smile.

I've got no body to go with!

This cartoon illustrates a classic joke. It adds to the humour of the joke, but it wouldn't be funny on its own.

Dangerous situations can make people laugh, when the only person to get hurt is a cartoon character!

Humour can come from overstating...

...or understating a character's reaction to a situation.

Some cartoons illustrate actual facts and people, but by taking things to extremes they can raise a smile.

Look closely at this cartoon and you'll see that it's making a humorous observation. The artist wants to show that dogs and their owners can often look alike – but the point is exaggerated and repeated to make you laugh.

Personification

One of the main techniques used by cartoonists is drawing animals or objects with human characteristics. This is called personification, and if you study what other artists do, you'll soon be able to do the same with your own drawings. All of the cartoons on this page have used human characteristics on non-human things.

Animals can wear clothes...

...or do human activities...

...or have human feelings and expressions.

Everyone knows who this is supposed to be, even though you'd never expect Santa to be a duck!

It's easy to make objects look human – just add eyes...

...or a face and limbs...

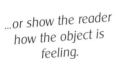

...or show the reader how the object is feeling.

Computers can think and communicate, so give them some personality, too.

Clever cartoons use features of the object as part of the process of becoming more human.

This cool cucumber would scare you if it ended up on your plate, but it's great for illustrating a common phrase!

Building Blocks

As you get better at drawing cartoons, you'll start to see that all things can be broken down into their basic shapes. Look at a pig, for instance, and you'll see that it's lots of circles making up the nose, face and body. Try copying your favourite TV cartoons by making them up out of shapes.

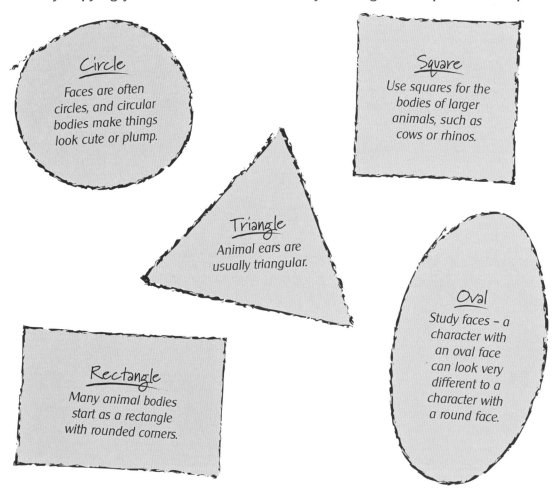

Circle
Faces are often circles, and circular bodies make things look cute or plump.

Square
Use squares for the bodies of larger animals, such as cows or rhinos.

Triangle
Animal ears are usually triangular.

Oval
Study faces – a character with an oval face can look very different to a character with a round face.

Rectangle
Many animal bodies start as a rectangle with rounded corners.

Shaping Up

Talented artists can look at any scene, person or animal and break it down into its basic shapes. Try studying the people around you, or pictures from your favourite books, and drawing them as a series of joined shapes. Then you can rework these shapes into cartoon characters.

These animals are all different shapes and sizes. Some are sitting, some are standing on two legs, and the fox is standing on four legs.

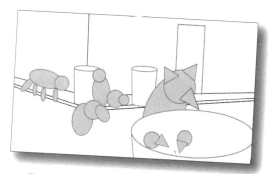

Take away the background details, and the animals can all be represented as body shapes.

Work up these outlines into a cartoon of the original drawing. The detail has gone, but the animals are still recognizable, and very appealing.

Speech and Sound

Many cartoons tell a story. If you want to use words in your cartoon, you should plan what to write before you draw your picture. That way, you can make sure you leave enough space for your words. Cartoonists use special shapes to show that their characters are saying the words.

This is a speech bubble. The tail part always points towards the person who is speaking.

Speech bubbles that are shaped like clouds contain thoughts or dreams.

Speech bubbles made of dashes shows that someone is whispering.

Speech bubbles with jagged edges indicate that the character is shouting.

Masterclass

Create different 'voices' for characters by using different styles of lettering

For example, you might want to use big, bold letters for a loud voice. Try looking on your PC for ideas for unusual fonts.

HELLO HELLO HELLO HELLO HELLO

Special Effects

Sometimes, you don't need to use speech bubbles to show what's going on in your cartoons. The words you write aren't always what people are saying. You can write noises and sounds instead.

Lost for words

A lightbulb above the head shows that the character has had an idea.

Wavy lines can illustrate surprise and horror.

Looks like this lady's in love.

Careful! This pizza's hot!

Seeing Sounds

Jagged lines in this cartoon show that the noise is loud, and emphasize who's making it.

Write any loud noises in big, bold letters.

Musical notes show someone is singing.

Lots of Zs shows this man's snoring.

Cartoon Colour

Colour can bring a cartoon to life, and there are loads of different ways to do it. The same cartoon sketch can look totally different when it's coloured using a different method.

Sketch

Crayon

Coloured pencil

Coloured pen

Paint

Digital

Shady Characters

Shading can add depth and interest to your cartoons. Try looking at objects in different kinds of light, and noticing which bits of them are in the shade. It doesn't have to be complicated – just a few lines or dots in the right place can make a difference.

Ink line sketch.

Hatching – use flicked or crossing lines to create shade.

Stipple – use lots of tiny dots close together to give the impression of darker tones.

Pencil – a quick way to add effective shading.

Ink wash – add water to ink to get different tones.

Digital – scan and shade on your PC.

Movement

The way you draw your characters will show what they're doing –
whether they're sitting down, standing up, or running around.
But cartoonists also add extra movement to pictures with tiny,
simple lines. They can show what direction the movements are
and how fast they are. Clever stuff, huh?

The lines above the horse show that he's thrown his rider headfirst into the cannon. Tiny lines suggest the rider's head is stuck!

This cowboy is clicking his heels as he jumps.

Hurray! This man's running and leaping because he's had a bright idea!

Masterclass

Make a reference book

Cartoons can show action in lots of different ways. Make a scrapbook containing lots of different styles of cartoons. Look for examples in comics, newspapers, books and magazines.

Use grand, swooping lines for big movements.

Lines are needed here to help show who's shooting who.

The lines show this witch has leapt off the ground in surprise!

Lines below show this man is jumping, not falling.

This picture looks much better with lines and a flash to show the boy has tripped.

Back to Basics

Starting Out

Ok, so it's time to start putting pencil to paper. These pages are full of loads of simple shapes that you can master in no time.

Expressions

Lots of books launch straight into telling you how to draw people – but let's face it, people are quite hard to draw! First practise drawing easier objects and making them into cartoon characters.

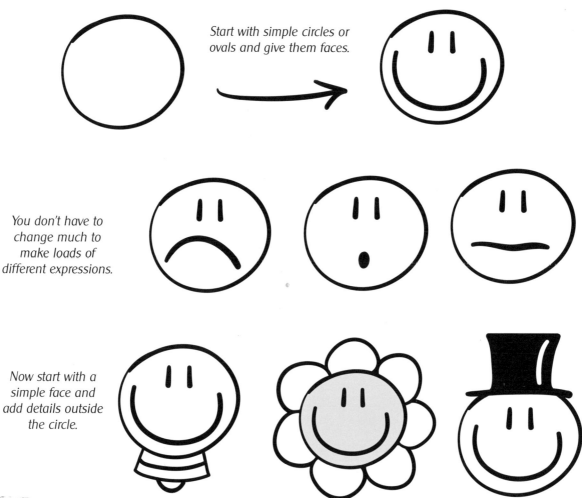

Start with simple circles or ovals and give them faces.

You don't have to change much to make loads of different expressions.

Now start with a simple face and add details outside the circle.

HAVE A GO !

How many expressions can you think of to draw? Use this space to come up with your own ideas.

 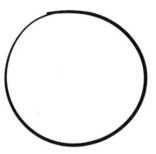 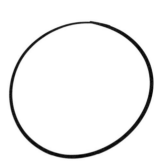

Planets

Now it's a simple progression to making actual objects. These planets are just circles with a bit more detail. They can show expressions, just like human faces. You can draw a whole range of crazy planet people!

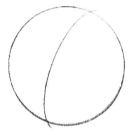

1. Start by drawing a freehand circle in pencil.

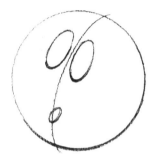

2. Add the eyes and mouth. These ones make it look scared.

3. Add some tiny extra lines for movement, and a bead of sweat.

4. Finally, colour it in. Show shadow on the underneath with a darker shade of the same colour.

Now draw more outlines and copy these first three smiling planets. They're all happy faces, but each planet looks different because of its colour. Now try drawing the one on the end – what do you think it's doing?

HAVE A GO !

Create your own solar system!
Here's some examples to get you going.

Stars and Rockets

Now it's time to add some life into your universe! Rockets can be simplified so they're really easy to draw. Even alien spaceships are just bubble shapes. And you can draw any kind of aliens you like inside – who's to say they don't look like that on the other side of the universe?!

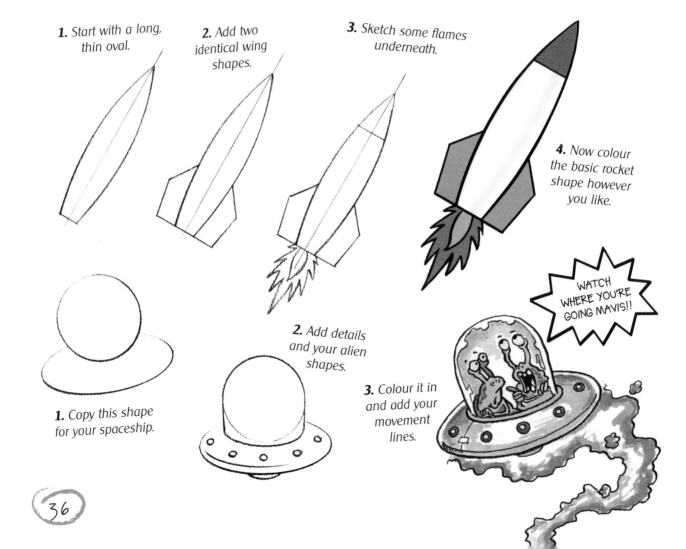

1. Start with a long, thin oval.

2. Add two identical wing shapes.

3. Sketch some flames underneath.

4. Now colour the basic rocket shape however you like.

1. Copy this shape for your spaceship.

2. Add details and your alien shapes.

3. Colour it in and add your movement lines.

WATCH WHERE YOU'RE GOING MAVIS!!

36

HAVE A GO!

Can you put a rocket into space?
Try drawing your own rocket among the
stars, or bring it into land on a far-off planet.

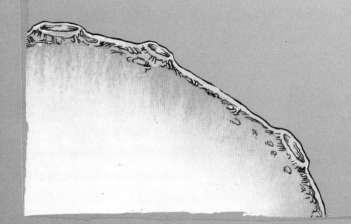

Buildings

Most of the people and animals you draw will look better with backgrounds behind them. Learn to draw some simple buildings – they're really only rectangles with faces on them!

1. This is the basic shape of a skyscraper.

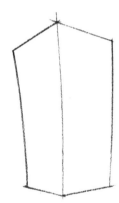

2. Add eyes and a smiling mouth.

3. Now put in a bit of shading. Don't forget the doors!

4. Finally, colour your building in.

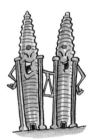

These famous skyscrapers look very happy today.

Make your buildings bend to give them more personality.

Add arms and legs to let your buildings really move!

Here's a space for you to draw your own cartoon street. Look at the one below for extra inspiration.

Make a cartoon version of your house – study it carefully first, and pick out details that make it yours.

Back to Nature

More easy shapes to bring your surroundings to life! Anything can be given a personality if you just add a smile or a frown, and maybe some arms or legs. Think about the characteristics of things. Would a volcano be grumpier than a mountain?

1. Trees are a combination of straight lines and circles.

2. Give the tree's leaves some texture and work out where the features should go.

3. Now add a few extra bits of detail and give your tree a happy expression.

4. Finally, add the colour. Remember, if it's autumn the leaves will be a different colour!

Remember humour – start with a mountain, then add eruption and a surprised look – voilà – a volcano!

Everyone can draw flowers – but you can add faces to show how they're feeling.

Try it with other things around you – start to study your surroundings more and you'll notice how different things can be – that's part of being a good cartoonist.

HAVE A GO !

Now take a walk outside and see what things you can draw in a cartoon style. Stick to simple shapes.

Keep it Simple

Now that you're gaining confidence, start to think of all the things you can draw already, then use your new cartoon style to make something more of them. Always keep your shapes simple at first.

All kinds of bugs are easy to draw – just add movement and expressions.

Even butterflies are simple, if they're more your thing.

Think of new things to try, like ghosts. They're so easy!

Masterclass

Make a flick book

Use an old notebook to make cartoons move! Draw a cartoon face on the bottom corner of the last page. Re-draw the face on the next page in, with its mouth slightly open. Then repeat with it open more, and so on until you have a sequence. Flick the corners of your book to make the mouth move.

HAVE A GO!

What could be scaring these creatures?
Can you draw a bigger, scarier creation?
Or just draw lots more frightened shapes
to practise the right expression.

Starting Out 43

COPY CATS

A library of simple shapes to get you started...

COPY
CATS

People Power

You're ready to try your hand at a cartoon person. Read on for the basics of creating a whole cast of characters and putting them into action.

Expressions

Faces

Body
Building

Hands
and Feet

Action

Features

Making Faces

Now for the 'real' stuff – drawing people. You've seen how professional cartoonists show different expressions. Let's start with a simple, smiling face with all the features in their normal place.

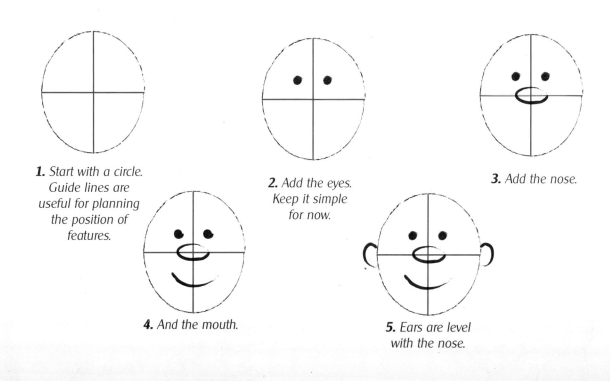

1. Start with a circle. Guide lines are useful for planning the position of features.

2. Add the eyes. Keep it simple for now.

3. Add the nose.

4. And the mouth.

5. Ears are level with the nose.

You can create different faces just by moving the features around.

HAVE A GO!

Moving the features closer or apart makes faces change. Try it on some of your own simple faces.

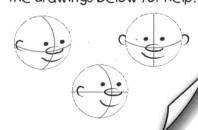

Masterclass

Features move around as a head turns to look in different directions

Have a go at drawing faces from different angles. Use the drawings below for help.

Features

Of course, you'll want to draw lots of different faces – old, young, fat, thin, round, long... You'll also want to add in hair and other features. These faces are all the same shape, but by changing the features you can make lots of different characters.

A baby might have small features and only a wisp of hair on its head.

Keep the beady eyes and add glasses, a bigger nose and a moustache, and you've got an old man.

This woman's features are just simple lines, but they make her look thoughtful, and a bit sad.

A toothy grin makes this boy look fun and cheeky. His nose and eyes are the same as the baby's, just a bit bigger.

This woman has harder features – angular glasses, beady eyes and pursed lips.

These faces all have different hair and features to give them their own personalities.

HAVE A GO !

Features can make people look very different. Try drawing cartoon family portraits in this space.

Emotions and Expressions

When drawing faces, you need to show what the character is feeling, too.
Study your own face in the mirror to see how it changes if it's angry,
surprised or sad. Try to draw the changes as you look at yourself.

*A happy,
relaxed face.*

*Take a happy
face, turn the
mouth down and
the eyebrows up,
and you've got a
sad face.*

*How does the
face change
when it's
surprised?*

*If you're really
angry, you
might frown
and grit your
teeth.*

*This boy is feeling
hot and bothered.*

*This woman is
dreaming.*

*This boy is
concentrating.*

*This girl looks
very snooty!*

*This boy is
crying with
laughter.*

Can you tell what these people are feeling? How many more expressions can you think of?

Building a Body

Now your faces need bodies. Look at real people – walking past,
on TV or in photos. You can see that they're all different proportions.
That means some are short and thin, some are tall and fat,
some have very long legs.

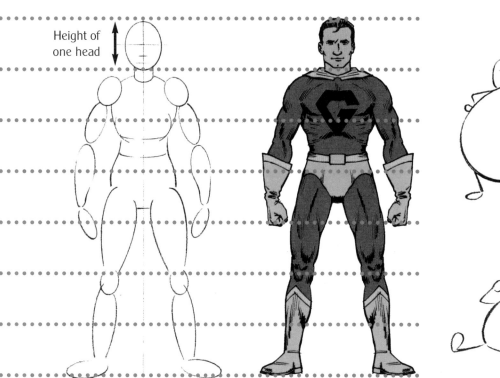

Height of
one head

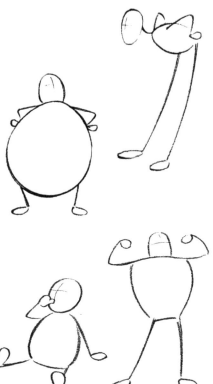

*First, learn to draw a correctly proportioned
body. Then you can alter the proportions to
make your characters look different.*

*Try drawing stick
figures with different
proportions.*

HAVE A GO !

Once you have mastered figures,
see how many poses you can put them in.

Little Extras

Once you've got the hang of the body, you need to master the 'fiddly bits' – the hands and feet. Many cartoonists simplify hands so they have fewer fingers, or no fingernails. See what works best for you.

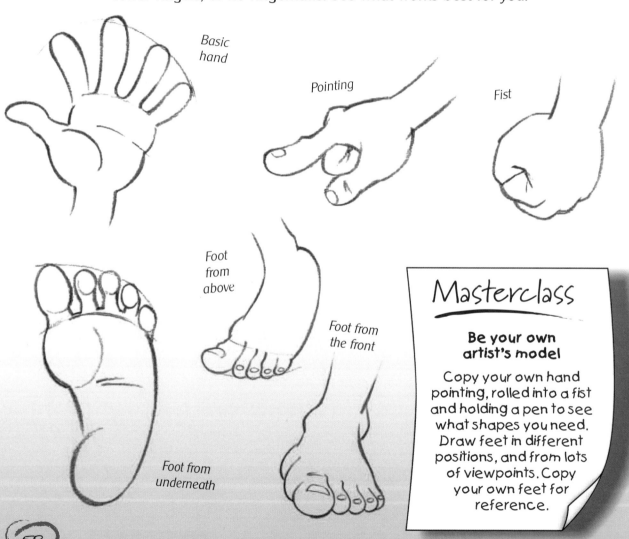

Basic hand

Pointing

Fist

Foot from above

Foot from the front

Foot from underneath

Masterclass

Be your own artist's model

Copy your own hand pointing, rolled into a fist and holding a pen to see what shapes you need. Draw feet in different positions, and from lots of viewpoints. Copy your own feet for reference.

HAVE A GO !

Of course, most feet you'll draw will usually have shoes on. The hands will be in motion.

Get Moving

Now you need to be able to make your people move convincingly. Let's start with walking and running. Turn your character sideways and let's get them on the go...

When you walk, you keep one foot on the ground. Your lifted leg swings forwards. Often, your arms swing at your sides.

When you start running, both feet leave the floor. Your arms swing higher and your legs move further apart.

HAVE A GO!

Add in movement lines and you can have people running about all over the place!

Notice how people run. If we're running away from something, we look different to when we're running towards something.

People Power 61

Lights, Camera, Action!

Let's find some more things for your characters to do. Study other artists' cartoons to see how they show movement. As you know, small lines can help, but you need to look at how people use their bodies to carry out different actions.

Even though this is a still picture, you can tell this man is fighting from the position of his arms, the expression on his face and the movement lines.

You can tell the characters are dancing, and it's made funnier by the long, swirling line that traces the path of the woman's movement.

This man is kicking a ball – look how he's leaning back to balance himself, with his arms moving to help him kick.

HAVE A GO!

Another page of things to have a look at and then try yourself. Can you find your favourite hobbies here, and draw people doing other things too?

COPY CATS

A library of people cartoons to get you started...

COPY CATS

COPY CATS

COPY CATS

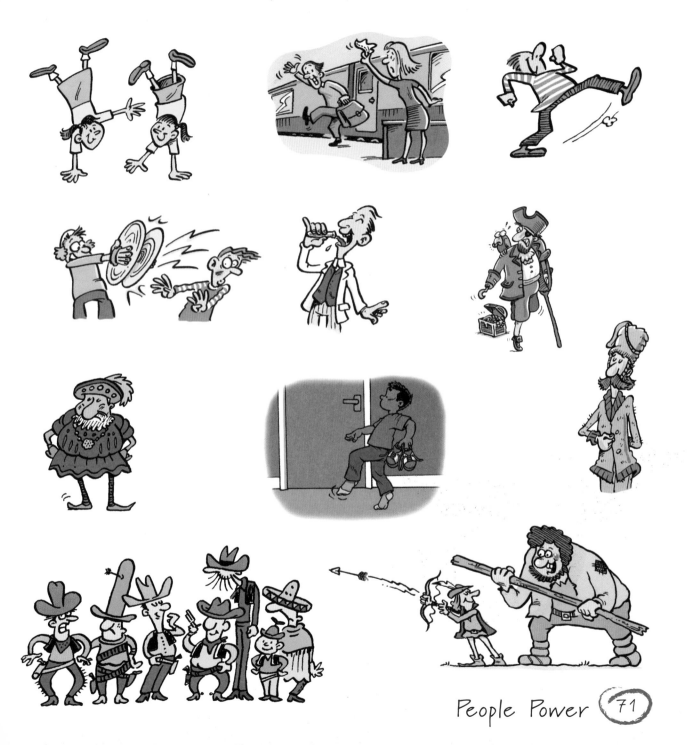

Animal Antics

In a cartoon, animals can have characters, opinions and voices, you can even see what they're thinking. Let your imagination run wild!

Basic
Shapes

Faces and
Expressions

Dinosaurs

Monsters

Movement

Basic Shapes

Start drawing animals in the same way as people – use a basic shape and then add movement and expressions. Unfortunately, there are more basic shapes than for humans!

Four-legged animals such as cows tend to have long, rectangular bodies with a leg at each corner. The head can be made from one or two circles. Add the markings and ears, and then colour it in.

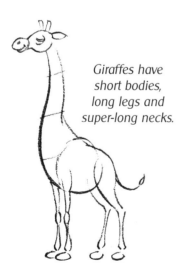

Giraffes have short bodies, long legs and super-long necks.

Horses are made of a collection of ovals and circles, but with straight, muscular legs.

Sheep are the basic four-legged shape, but nice and easy – like clouds with legs.

HAVE A GO!

It doesn't matter how exotic an animal, you can still start with the same shapes. Work from the ones on the left-hand page to make these, and other animals.

Strike a Pose

And what if it's not standing on four legs? You can draw animals in all kinds of positions – still by breaking them down into shapes. The animals shown below are made from a collection of ovals and triangles – or a combination of both.

A walrus is an oval with tail, fins and tusks added.

Most birds are made up of circles for the body and head, with a tail.

This panda is just a circle with legs and arms!

Some four-legged animals sit on their hind legs. Use circles to create the basic shape.

HAVE A GO !

See if you can spot the basic shapes making these animals, then try drawing them next to the finished versions.

On the Move

You could practise drawing animals standing around until the cows come home, but for real cartoons you'll need to set them in motion. Like people, you can move their arms, legs and heads and add action lines.

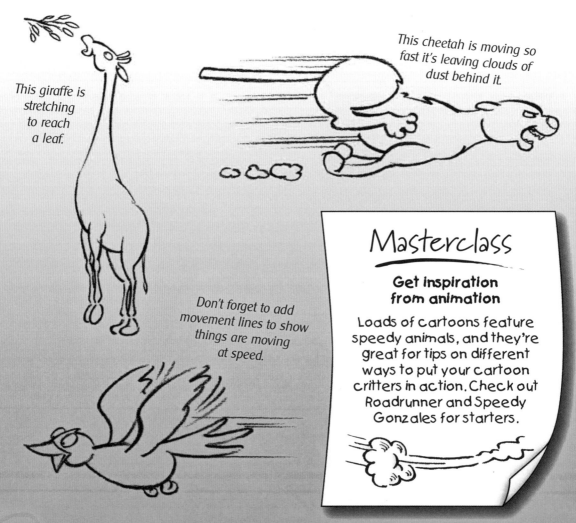

This giraffe is stretching to reach a leaf.

This cheetah is moving so fast it's leaving clouds of dust behind it.

Don't forget to add movement lines to show things are moving at speed.

Masterclass

Get inspiration from animation

Loads of cartoons feature speedy animals, and they're great for tips on different ways to put your cartoon critters in action. Check out Roadrunner and Speedy Gonzales for starters.

HAVE A GO!

Can you tell what it is about these animals that makes them look as though they are moving? Try drawing your own examples using these techniques.

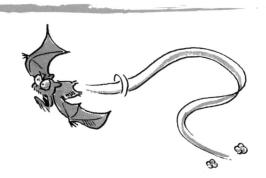

Faces and Expressions

Don't forget that in cartoons you can make animals more like people.
They can wear clothes, walk on two legs, or have emotions.
Some animals can be sad-looking, or angry.

Slumped shoulders and a wrinkled brow make this chimp look glum.

This pig's on the run – he looks alarmed!

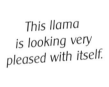

This llama is looking very pleased with itself.

Scary eyes and a twitching tail make this squirrel look like he's smelled something bad!

This creature has had a bit of a shock. He's even sweating!

The extra lines and shapes make this rabbit look hopping mad.

But here's a happy fellow, with such a big grin his eyes have closed.

HAVE A GO!

In cartoons, animals can think and even talk. Try adding speech or thought bubbles to the animals on this page. Use the space to come up with your own ideas.

Animal Antics

Dinosaurs

Dinosaurs are animals that died out a long time ago. You still draw them in the same way. They, too, start as basic shapes, with added spikes, scales and teeth.

Most meat eaters walked on two legs. Start this one with a triangle.

Use two circles here, then add Triceratops' distinguishing features.

Add a looong neck and tail to an oval for leaf eaters.

Use a semi-circle with a head and tail for Stegosaurus.

HAVE A GO !

It's easiest to draw dinosaurs if you study pictures of them. Take your fave characters and turn them into cute cartoons or scarier creations.

Making Monsters

Now you're getting the hang of this, let your imagination run riot.
Think of all the other creatures you can start to draw. How about
some prehistoric friends for your dinosaurs?

*Once you have
mastered dinosaurs,
you can easily
turn them into
monsters.*

*Or just make
your tiger's teeth
larger to create a
sabre-toothed variety.*

*Many prehistoric creatures
are similar to animals we
see today. Learn how to
draw fur, and you can
turn an elephant into
a mammoth!*

*All you need is a little
imagination... or a lot
of heads and necks!*

HAVE A GO !

What has scared this person? Try drawing your
own terror-worthy monster in the space below.

COPY CATS

A library of animal cartoons to get you started...

COPY CATS

COPY
CATS

COPY CATS

Making a Scene

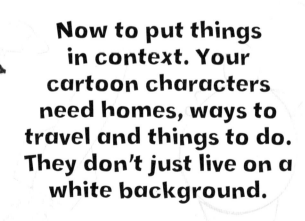

Now to put things in context. Your cartoon characters need homes, ways to travel and things to do. They don't just live on a white background.

Getting Around

Props

Scenes

Landscapes

Clothes and Props

People's clothes tell you a lot about them. Are they living nowadays, or in a historical time? Are they doing a particular job with a uniform? Things that they're carrying or holding can also give you clues to who they are and what they do. What can you tell about each of these characters?

Doctors are usually dressed in white. This one has good news!

What is it about this character that tells us he is not a modern-day soldier?

Pirates are often drawn wearing eyepatches. All this guy's missing is a parrot on his shoulder!

Look how much energy and aggression this sportsman has!

You'll probably need to copy photos to get uniforms and equipment right.

HAVE A GO!

Can you finish off the cartoons below? Look at what the tennis player is wearing, then draw a rival player. Can you sketch a fearsome opponent for the Viking?

Making a Scene

Getting Around

Your cartoon people need to travel around, and cars, trains and planes can make exciting action scenes. Look how the wheels change to ovals to show they're moving. Shapes look like they become a bit stretched when they're moving fast. Don't forget to add smoke, steam and action lines.

Everyone knows that aeroplanes have to fly fast to stay up in the air, so all the artist has added here are a few puffs of cloud.

This train must be travelling fast – the artist has drawn it sloping backwards slightly. Bits of its cargo are flying up in the air, too!

The wheels of this car have changed to ovals, and the cloud of smoke makes the cartoon funny.

HAVE A GO!

Of course, cars aren't the only way to get around. How do you want your cartoon characters to travel?

Landscapes

Now you've been drawing for so long, it's time to put together all the things you know, to make a whole cartoon scene. Think hard about where you want your characters to appear, as well as what you want them to look like.

The easiest background is made by just adding a horizon line.

Adding a few more details to the horizon and a sky above completes the scene.

Different details in the background will show where the character is.

Adding silhouettes behind the main action is a good way to introduce depth to your cartoons.

When your scene is more complicated, you'll need a more detailed background.

HAVE A GO !

Create your own landscape. What about drawing someone on the moon, or in the jungle? Try to add something funny to make people look closely.

Inside and Out

If you're setting your cartoon indoors, you can either use a couple of props to set the scene, or draw more detail in the background. Think of how you'd draw all the things in your home.

Sketch the basic shapes, like the TV, chair and people, before you add more detail to this scene.

There's lots going on in this picture! Make sure you allow enough space for all the details.

Draw your outlines in faint pencil first. Then you can rub out things that don't show, like the character behind the ironing board...

Even though this scene takes place indoors, there's still loads of action to draw.

...or the desk hidden by your character.

HAVE A GO !

Try drawing different objects and places around your house.

Masterclass

Can you draw your bedroom in a cartoon style?

Remember, just sketch the basic shape and add in any important features. It's often easiest to start with big things, like wardrobes or beds, and and then add the little details.

COPY CATS

A library of extra bits to get you started...

COPY CATS

COPY
CATS

Put into Practice

This is the place to test out your new-found skills. These pages have projects and games to develop your cartooning techniques.

Final Touches

Make Your Own Strip

How Cartoon Strips Work

Finishing Off

Text Effects

Thank You Notes

Final Touches

Before you progress to drawing cartoon strips, it's a good idea to practise different colouring and shading techniques. The examples below show different ways of treating the same characters, just by using colour and shading. Try it yourself on the cartoons on the right.

Only using colour...

Only using shading...

Using both colour and shading.

Add shading...

Add colour...

Add colour...

Add colour...

In Other Words

Speech bubbles come in all shapes and sizes, and you'll need lots of different kinds to show what your characters are saying and thinking. Can you come up with words that fit the speech and thought bubbles on these pages?

Cartoon Strips

Now start putting your cartooning skills together to make a strip. Study the comic strip below. Each of the scenes is drawn in its own box. Typically, cartoon strips have three or four panels, but this is not a rule – as many as the story or joke needs and space allows is fine.

The first panel of a cartoon strip sets the scene and introduces the characters. It's best to keep things simple, because you'll have to re-draw characters and scenes several times to make a whole strip.

Tiny lines show he's shaking his head

Panel 2 develops the story and characters. The key to this development is the contrast between the increasingly dramatic and noisy driver and his silent but expressive passenger.

Consider how much space you will need in your speech bubble and allow for this space when planning your composition

The scream follows the path of the hill to highlight the sense of speed

Movement lines and dust show that something (the cart) has just shot out of the frame very quickly

By panel 3 it is clear that the passenger does not share his friend's enthusiasm. His eyes are wide and his body is rigid with fear. The humour is heightened by the fact that his friend is oblivious to his distress.

The final part delivers the 'punchline' of the story. Sam has opted out of the 'deadly feat' but has ensured his friend can't stick around to convince him otherwise. Sam cheekily puts on an innocent look – he isn't reacting to his friend's scream, his hands are behind his back and he's whistling.

Do it Yourself

Now it's your turn! Use these frames to draw your own cartoon strip. Practise first on scrap paper so you're sure your story fits into the correct number of boxes. If you're stuck for ideas, choose your favourite from these:

Bullying Lesson

1. A boy is walking to school.

2. A bully jumps out to make boy jump.

3. Just around the corner, a monster jumps out...

4. ...and makes the bully REALLY jump!

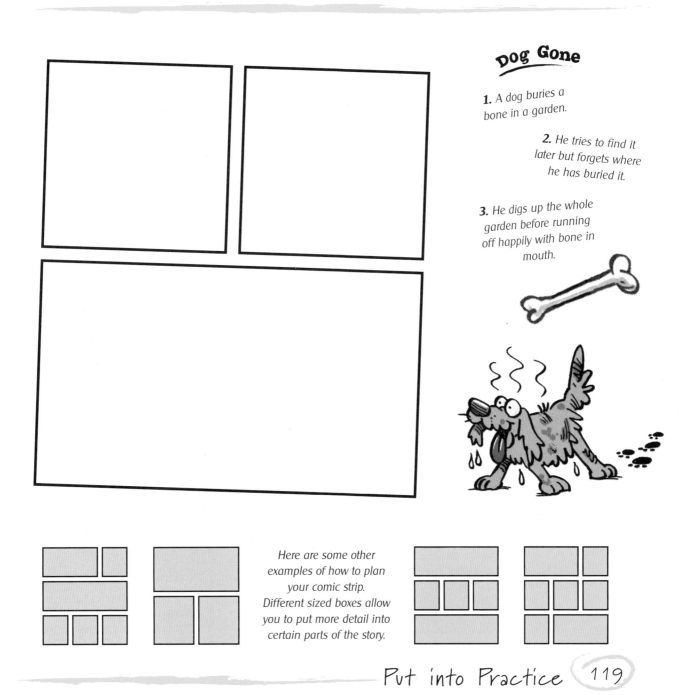

Dog Gone

1. A dog buries a bone in a garden.

2. He tries to find it later but forgets where he has buried it.

3. He digs up the whole garden before running off happily with bone in mouth.

Here are some other examples of how to plan your comic strip. Different sized boxes allow you to put more detail into certain parts of the story.

Thank You!

Now you're an ace artist, you can design your own stationery, too. Use your favourite characters and animals to make birthday cards and postcards to send to your friends. Design your own thank-you notes, with your artwork at the top, and you'll be able to get away with writing shorter letters. People will be so impressed with your art skills, they'll hardly notice what you've written underneath!

1. *Buy a notebook with plain paper in it, or cut printer paper neatly in half to make smaller sheets.*

2. *Carefully draw your chosen design at the top or bottom of the page. Make sure it fills a third of the page or less.*

3. *Colour it in, and copy the design onto the bottom corner of your envelope, too. Very professional!*

Dear Grandma,

Thank you so much for my wonderful present.

I had a great party!

Love from Tommy xx

Happy holiday

Thank you for gifts

Party invitation

Get well soon

Moving house

Finishing Off

Now that you've mastered pen and paper, use your imagination to finish off the cartoons below. Go as wild as you like!

What do you see in the mirror?

What is this king riding?

What is on this man's tray?

Who's going over the Niagara Falls in a barrel?

Which animal is chasing this cat?

What is this man juggling?

Who has won the race?

Add another duckling.

Masterclass

A cartoon consequences game to play with a couple of friends

Draw a cartoon head at the top of a piece of paper. Fold the paper to hide what you've drawn, and ask a friend to draw the body. The next person draws the legs. Open it up to see what kind of cartoon creature you've created.

Some pages for you to sketch in

Some pages for
you to sketch in

Some pages for
you to sketch in

Some pages for
you to sketch in

Some pages for
you to sketch in

Some pages for you to sketch in

Some pages for
you to sketch in

Some pages for
you to sketch in

Some pages for
you to sketch in

Some pages for
you to sketch in

Acknowledgements

*The publishers wish to thank the following artists
who have contributed to this book:*

**Mike Foster at The Maltings Partnership
Tom Slemmings
Cover artwork Mark Davis**

All other artworks come from Miles Kelly Archives.

*The publishers would like to thank the following
sources for the use of their photographs:*

p 9 t/r TOM AND JERRY © Warner Bros/pictorialpress.com
p 9 b/l SCOOBY © Hanna-Barbera/pictorialpress.com
p 10 l SUPERMAN © Marvel Comics/pictorialpress.com
p 11 t/r SIMPSONS © Fox TV/pictorialpress.com
p 11 b/l SHREK © DreamWorks/pictorialpress.com
p 17 b/l KIKI © Buena Vista/pictorialpress.com